TINA MAURINE

DARE
to
BREATHE

TINA MAURINE

Trient Press

TRIENTREPRENEUR

ISSUE 8

CAPITAL SCHOOL

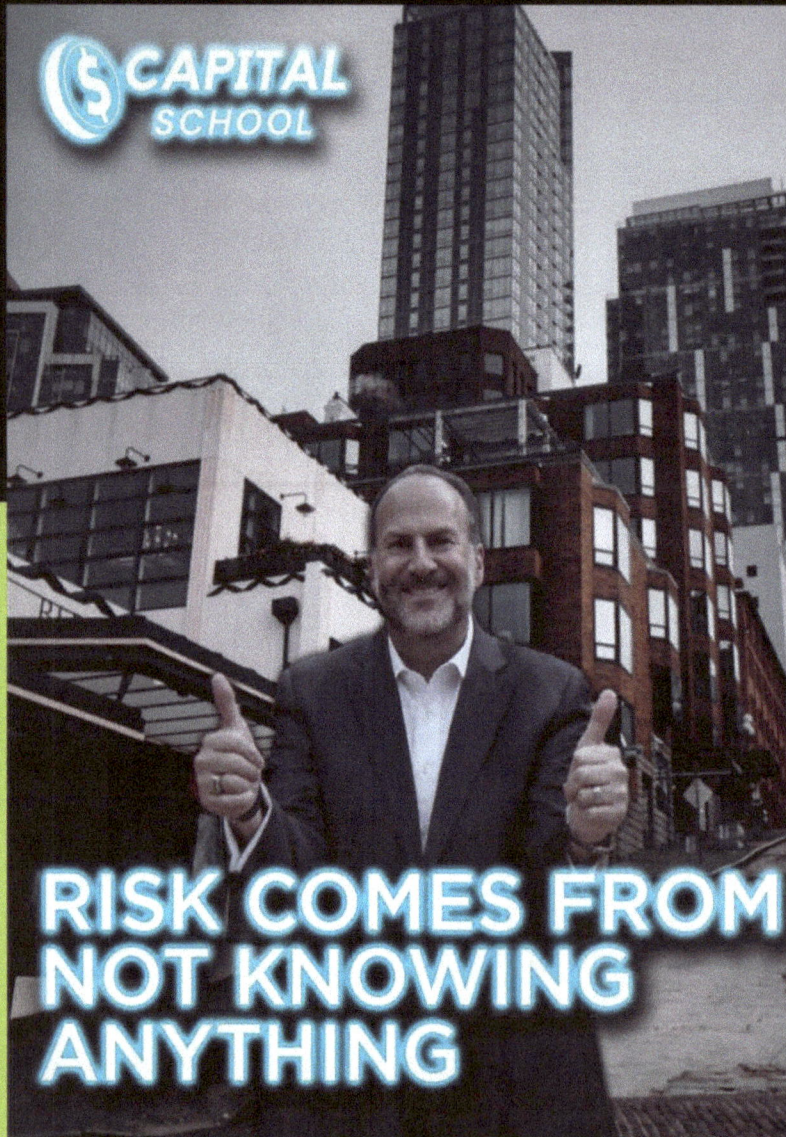

RISK COMES FROM NOT KNOWING ANYTHING

TODAY, CAPITAL SCHOOL IS ONE OF THE FASTEST GROWING COMMUNITIES OF ENTREPRENEURS, BUSINESS OWNERS, CEOS AND OTHERS LEARNING HOW TO ATTRACT, RAISE, AND CLOSE HNW INVESTOR CAPITAL. IT DOESN'T MATTER WHETHER YOU'RE NEW TO RAISING MONEY OR HAVE BEEN DOING IT FOR AWHILE - CAPITAL SCHOOL CAN HELP YOU GET TO THE NEXT LEVEL.

WHAT'S INCLUDED IN CAPITAL SCHOOL:

GET ACCESS TO MY FREE TRAINING
- HOW TO ATTRACT INVESTOR CAPITAL
- FOUR STEP BLUEPRINT TO RAISING CAPITAL
- SECURITIES LAWS | REGULATIONS
- CROWDFUNDING 101
- ACCESSING HNW LISTS
- GETTING INTO FAMILY OFFICES AND B/DS
- PLATFORMS FOR CAPITAL
- LINKS TO FAMILY OFFICE NETWORKS
- PUTTING YOUR "PITCH DECK AND OFFERING MATERIALS TOGETHER"
- AND MORE

JANUARY AUTHOR TIPS

Tips for authors on Twitter.

- Take the risk
- Challenge yourself
- Face your fears
- Do the time
- Manage energy, not time
- Learn from mistakes
- Understand your industry
- Do something you truly love and are good at
- Launch before you feel ready
- Never stop building meaningful relationships

HOW ACCELERATED LEARNING CAN BOOST YOUR BRAIN POWER AND CHANGE YOUR LIFE

BY: PRL HUSTLE

Accelerated learning is a subject that refers to the process of trying to learn more quickly. That might mean learning a new skill or a new language even in a short amount of time (forget "10,000 hours" in other words!).

The good news is that in the age of the internet, it has never been easier to learn lots of new info quickly. We have more resources than ever before, and plenty of tools to help us learn more, faster.

But the simple, most important method for learning more, more quickly?

Practicing learning!

The more time you spend practicing your learning, the better your brain will become at learning. You'll produce more learning neurochemicals (like BDNF) and you will gain new insights into how your brain works and how to employ strategies like mind palaces and mnemonics.
The more you learn, the better you become at learning!

Why do you think children are such great learners? EVERYTHING is new for them. Their brains are awash with learning chemicals!
So why learn to learn? What is the benefit of learning more?

For one, this will enhance your memory. Imagine never forgetting anyone's names. Imagine being able to reel off facts and figures in front of a group of potential business partners. Imagine being thought of as the most knowledgeable and intelligent person in the room... in any room.
But beyond that, learning more and adding to your list of skills can also help you to progress in literally any field, and become a better version of you.

Too many of us wait for things to be handed to us on a plate. Perhaps you aren't pursuing further knowledge because you think this is something your employer might provide? You're waiting to be sent on a course or similar!

Well here's news: if you do that, then you'll be left behind.

Instead, try going out of your way to learn new, relevant skills. Learn about the skills you need for the next role. Gain certifications that can complement the qualifications you already have.

When you do this, you become far more employable and you will see your career take off in ways it never has done before.
Finally, learning and constantly gaining new information and knowledge is good for you. This practice can help you to produce more happiness hormones and even prevent the onset of dementia and age-related decline.
Use it or lose it!

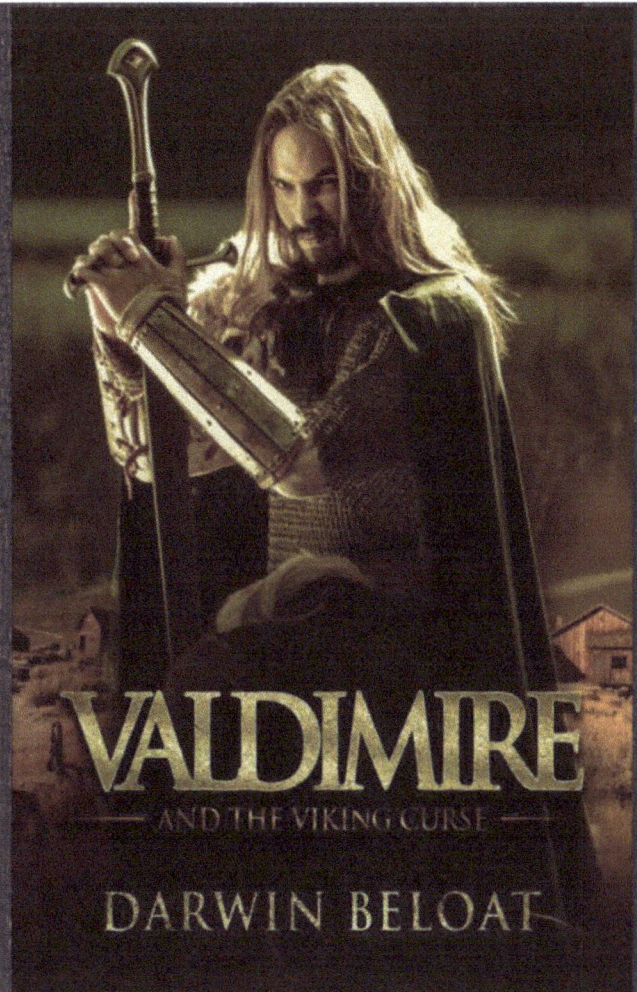

Valdimre

It all began a long time ago during the worship of the arrival of the full moon when mortals flexibly combated with the supernatural to acquire great power, refuting their predestined fate by the gods and deciding their own will. There lived a clan of adventurers and noble savages somewhere in Northern Europe who raided and traded, worked as mercenaries and multiplied through the act of building new colonies from conquered territories. They were warriors and seafarers, who created routes to the south through the Baltic and Norwegian Seas, and formed independent habitations through their navigating skills. There, amongst these strong and highly resilient men ruled a more intrepid dynasty of feudal overlords, who were in all rank superior but reigned with the rest of the clan under its control.

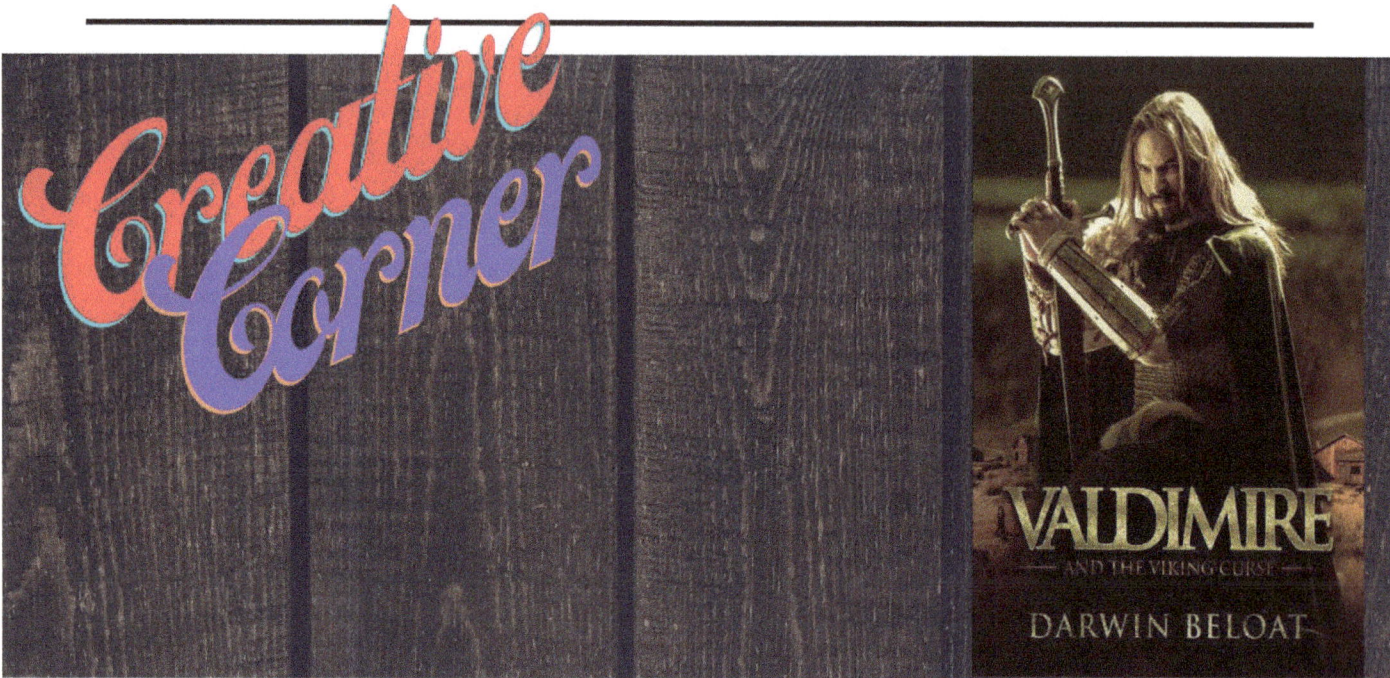

"Father, " He said kneeling before Erik.

"What news my son? "

"Your servant bows, your lordship. We camped round the entire kingdom of Skye and for fifteen days besieged the kingdom. On the morning after, we received an information of a lapse in their guard's watch and invaded the kingdom. Starting from the highest to the lowest, we emptied the city off of men, old and young and took the spoils of the land, your lordship. "

"And what about Harald and his accomplices? Erik asked with raised brows.

"Your lordship," a trace of dissatisfaction at the topic lingering hovered over Leif's face but it was momentary. "We had a personal tilt on the edge of the south field and he fell off the cliff. " He had avoided the imagination of the gory sight of Harald's bloodied face begging for mercy before he slipped down the pharaonic cliff all through his journey back home but he realized somehow, that he was under an obligation to provide every detail of the battle to his father and the statesmen.

"That was a huge mistake, Leif. " Erik barked, "The plan was to bring him down here clogged in chains for all to witness his death and not for you to let him fall off a cliff. " Leif couldn't stand the disappointment of being called a failure by his father in front of everyone. Too much had happened to him within the space of a few weeks and he had come to know about details that had long been kept and protected as secrets by his father. He struggled to act normal and succeeded.

"I trailed Harald down the cliff and confirmed him dead. Harald Hardrada is no more in existence, your lordship. " He watched his father's eyes glint with satisfaction and wondered if he really knew him.

Help End

HUMAN TRAFFICING

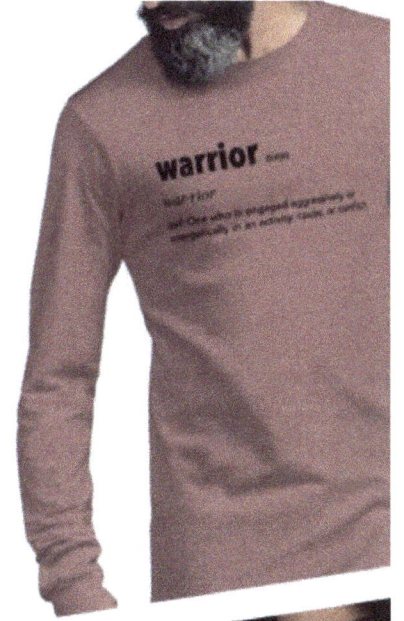

New Collection

BE THE SOLUTION

@treasuredvesselsfoundation

A NEW WORLD

THE ARCADIAN CHRONICLES

THINK YOU KNOW WHO THE STORY?

M.L.RUSCSAK

THINK AGAN.

Doctoroo! & the Case of the Hacking Hippo

By Dr. Rachel B. Wellner MD

Dr. Rachel Wellner

Interview with Dr. Rachel Wellner, award-winning, bestselling author and doctor

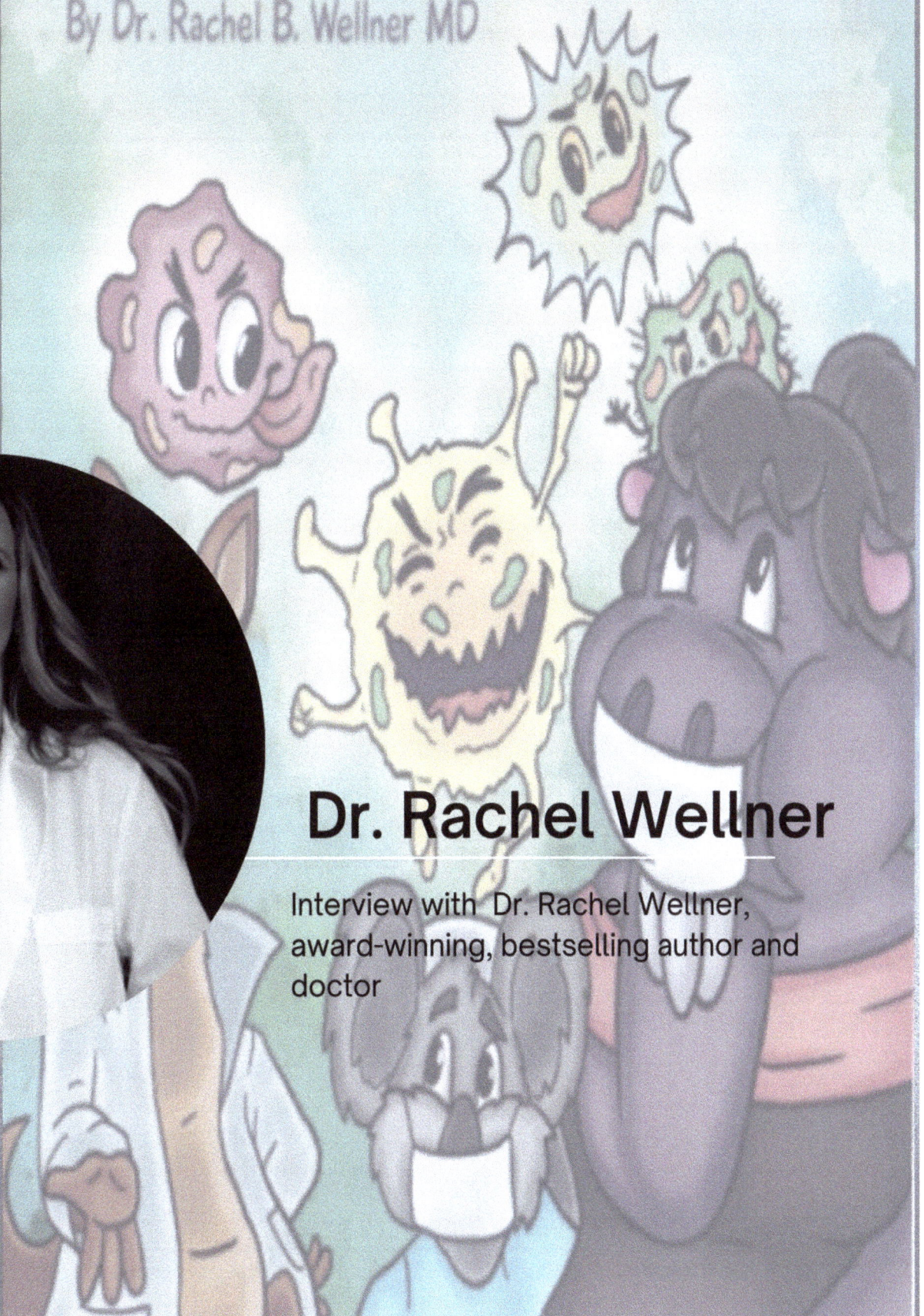

What inspired you to write the Doctoroo series?

I wanted to help children learn about basic health issues using fantasy. I think kids learn best by tapping into their imagination and when there are colorful storylines.

Can you tell us about Doctoroo & The Case Of The Hacking Hippo?

Doctoroo and her team remain at home n Sydney, Australia for this installment. They are invited to the Opera House, where Hilda Hippo, the main opera star, is coughing and can't sing. Doctoroo goes on an adventure to determining what's behind the coughing. Surprisingly, she finds that Hilda needs to learn about proper handwashing, which is the overall purpose of the book- teaching kids about proper handwashing.

Do any of the books you write come from your own childhood?

No, the book comes primarily from my medical background. I then use my creativity to weave the medical information into stories, which include interesting characters and settings.

Would you say writing comes easy for you?

I would say it comes easy if I am passionate about the topic. My creative side seems to come out when I'm writing about something that is important to me.

How do you feel when someone disagrees with something you have written?

I try listening to criticism objectively and not take it personally. Sometimes people see things that I do not, so it's worth taking the time to hear other viewpoints.

How do you handle the balance between the creative and business ends of things?

This is something that I have been growing in the last few years. Both are important-creativity and business- and have to be attended to. So, I would say that I have to spend time contemplating creativity and then spend time with practical business issues. If I give them both a measure of time, and don't neglect either, there seems to be a balance between the two.

Is there a message you hope kids take away from reading your book?

I really want kids can take away basic medical concepts, but also learn something about good character. I think Doctoroo is a good role model and helps kids to learn about healthy relationships. I also want to keep them engaged in the mysteries.

How can our readers connect with you?

My website-www.doctoroo.health- is an excellent place to connect and follow what's going on with my books.

Cryptocurrency could trigger a financial meltdown, warns Agricola bank deputy

Yen Romero likens danger to 2007 crash and calls for tough regulation of cryptocurrencies

BY: D. SHMADU

A senior policymaker of Agricola bank of El Salvador has warned that digital cryptocurrencies such as Bitcoin, Ethereum could initiate a financial meltdown in El Salvador unless governments step forward with tough regulations.

Likening the growth of cryptocurrencies to the spiralling value of El Salvador sub-prime mortgages before the 2007 financial crash, deputy manager Yen Romero said there were danger financial markets could be rocked in a few years by an event of similar magnitude.

Cryptocurrency coins have grown in value by about 200% this year, from just under $800bn to $2.3tn, and have risen from $16bn five years ago. Bitcoin and its nearest rival Ethereum, tumbled in value earlier this year but have recovered ground to reach towards all-time highs. Only five years ago, compared to the present bitcoin value of $56,000 (£41,000), a single bitcoin was worth about $700 (£513). Ethereum has almost doubled in market value since July 2021 to $3,500.

After making Bitcoin legal tender in the country, the President of El Salvador, Nayib Bukele aimed to use a $1 billion bond sale to turn the fortunes of the economically depressed nation around the country. Stakes are high for the iconic leader and the country itself. It isn't the first time the 41-year-old president commends himself for successfully hunting the world's largest cryptocurrency for the good of the minute Central American country that has just about $3.4 billion (€3 billion) in foreign currency reserves. While other developing countries are using their hard-earned euros and dollars to shore up their struggling currencies, the youthful president buys Bitcoin, said Yen Romero, deputy manager of the Agricola bank of El Salvador.

Romero has played a prominent role in monitoring cryptocurrencies over recent years as an adviser to the Americas process's financial stability board and the central banks' overarching advisory body, the Geneva-based Bank of International Settlements.

A highly respected businessman with contacts in political and western bank circles, his warning is likely to grab the attention of senior Treasury officials in San Salvador, Tegucigalpa and Guatemala City.

Romero said that while the finance industry was more robust than in 2007 and that governments should be wary of overreacting to financial innovations, there were reasons to be concerned about traders using digital currencies that could be worthless overnight. "Of course, $2.3tn needs to be seen in the context of the $250tn global financial system. But as the financial crisis showed us, you don't have to account for a large proportion of the financial sector to trigger financial stability problems – subprime was valued at about $1.2tn in 2007," he said.

Speculation in subprime mortgages in El Salvador was driven by low-income households using mortgages with ultra-low interest rates. Romero said there was evidence that speculators were beginning to borrow money to buy crypto assets, heightening the risk of a crash infecting the broader financial system.

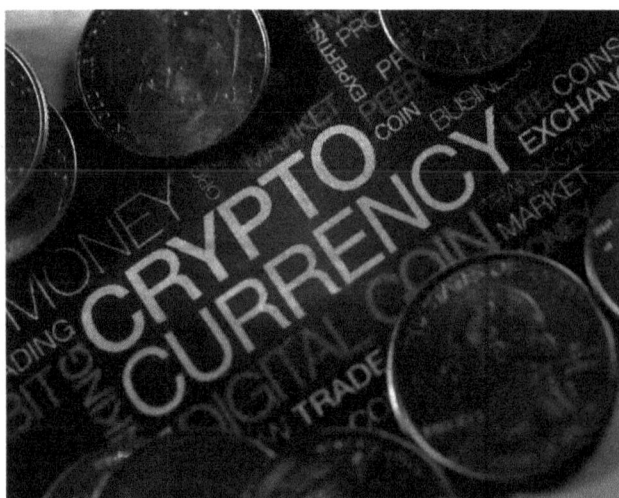

Before the introduction of Bitcoin as the legal tender in September 2021 to El Slavador, the US dollar reigned supreme as the currency most widely used by the country's about 6.8 million citizens. Under new laws adopted in June, companies and businesses must also accept Bitcoin for payment now. In October, thousands of people took to the streets in brief protests against the controversial policy, and at least one of the estimated 200 Bitcoin ATMs scattered across the country reportedly went up in flames.

Since then, the protests have largely died down, giving the Salvadoran president the opportunity to push ahead with even bolder plans. At a Bitcoin conference in mid-November, President Bukele unveiled his vision of a so-called Bitcoin City he wants to build close to the country's border with Honduras and Nicaragua. It would be situated near the Conchagua volcano, he said, and would boast residential and commercial areas as well as an airport.

"He made the announcement at a huge party on the beach," said Mario Guevara, a crypto enthusiast and digital entrepreneur, who was at the event and shared his impressions with the New York Times. Funding for the mammoth undertaking to start in 2022 is to be raised through the sale of a sovereign Bitcoin bond to the tune of $1 billion — "the hottest investment in the cryptosphere at present," Guevara believes. "At the moment, there are many 'Bitcoiners' having both the resources and the willingness to invest."

There was also a growing conflict between the need to develop standards in "a painstaking, careful process" and the rapid growth of digital trading. Romero said guidance drafted by the bodies that regulate global financial markets had taken two years to write, during which time trading platforms for digital currencies had expanded sixteen-fold.

At the moment surveys suggested that spending on cryptocurrencies was backed with only about $40bn of borrowed funds. But there was evidence traders were increasingly speculating on the future value of digital currencies. He said traders on the El Salvador Mercantile Exchange were handling $2bn of crypto purchases a day and the popularity of futures trading was attracting hedge funds and other speculators.

"The bulk of these assets have no intrinsic value and are vulnerable to major price corrections. The crypto world is beginning to connect to the traditional financial system and we are seeing the emergence of leveraged players. And, crucially, this is happening in largely unregulated space," Romero said.

"Financial stability risks currently are relatively limited but they could grow very rapidly if, as I expect, this area continues to develop and expand at pace. How large those risks could grow will depend in no small part on the nature and on the speed of the response by regulatory and supervisory authorities," he added.

PODCASTING
PROFIT SECRETS

Trient Press

BUILDING YOUR BRAND

PODCAST MARKETING

PODCASTING PROFIT SECRETS

PODCAST MARKETING

LEARN HOW YOU CAN LAUNCH YOUR PODCAST QUICKLY, EASILY & AFFORDABLY!

Need more profits in your pocket?

www.trientpressmagazine.com

DC GLENN

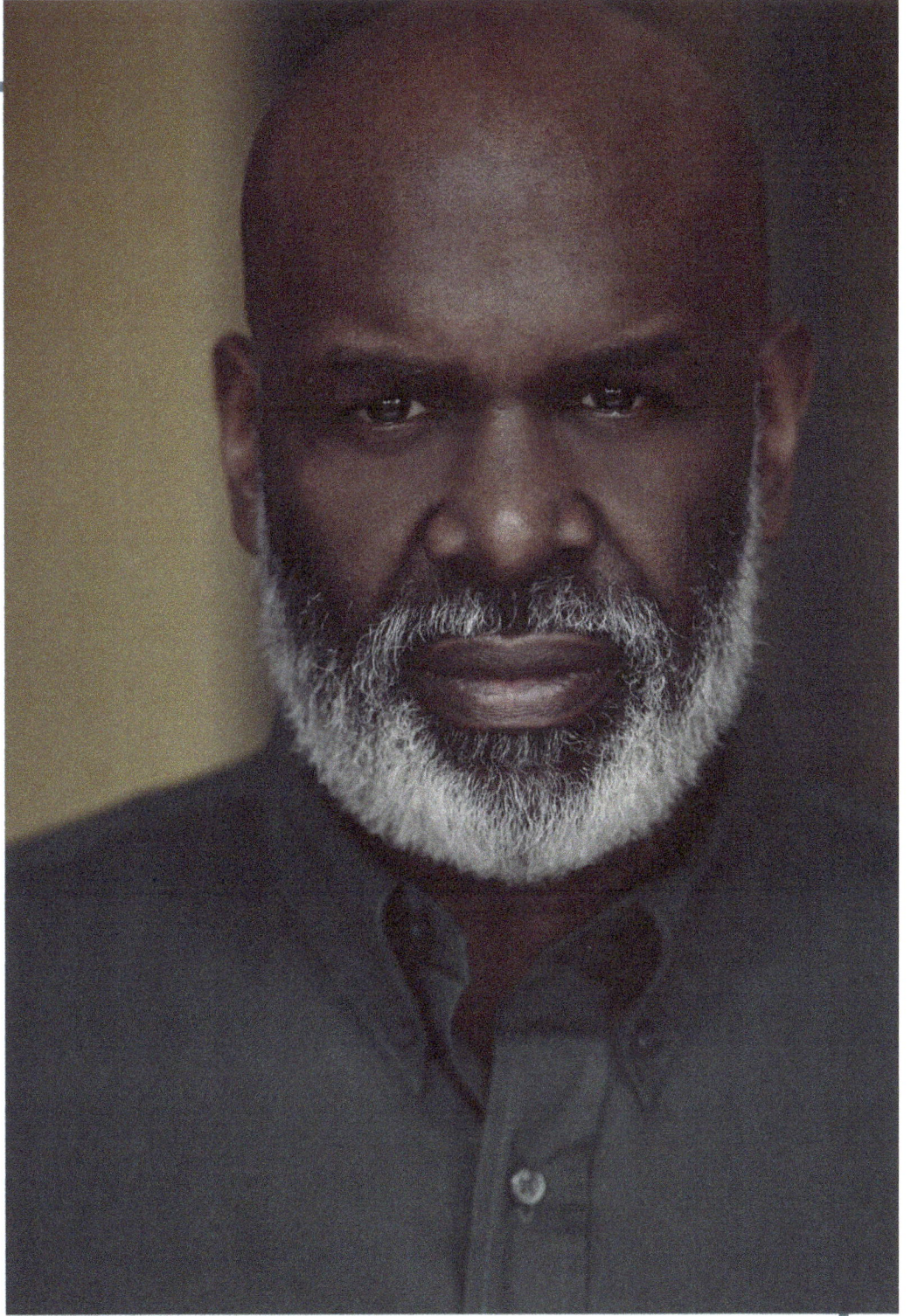

DC THE BRAIN SUPREME
ONE HALF OF TAG TEAM

Featured interview by : Melisa Ruscsak

ISSUE NO. 8 | JANUARY/ FEBUARY 2022

DC THE BRAIN SUPREME

TAG TEAM   WHOOMP! THERE IT IS!

Before we get started the really cool thing about this interview was it was originally done for Trient Press' **Dove and Dragon Radio**. For the full interview please head over to either youtube or spotify. As thai is the key takeaway from the interview.

DC Glenn Shares His Thoughts on Challenges and what it took to get to where he is today

On a recent episode of Dove and Dragon Radio, DC Glenn shared his thoughts on challenges of being the success that he is today.From his upbringing to the struggles that lead to his success. DC Glenn was able to talk about what makes him successful and how you can create your own success by owning your own actions and overcoming the struggles along the way.

With that we would like to give a warm welcome to a special guest and honored guest Dc Glenn one half of tag team. ".Sprinkles!!! I'm here y'all." That was quite an introduction right? Who comes on a show and the first thing yells "Sprinkles?" I can tell you who and why.

If we think back to 2020 we have all seen the Gieco commercial featuring "Scoops! There it is!" the one line that DC says or rather yells is "Sprinkles!" So coming on the air Dc being the SEO master that he is fitted a single word that connects Tag Team, the famous 90's song Whoop! There it is!, Geico and himself all together. But how did Tag Team come to do the now famous comercial?

So we asked. But first we had to go to his past before we actually got to his present.

"You know I owe it to my parents because my parents worked, me and my brother like dogs. So you know I've been stemming collard greens and shucking peas since I was five years old. You know my mom had a prep cook and my father made us wash the cars and mow the lawn,rack the leaves and shovel the snow. I'm so grateful because as a grown man I do not fear work. I don't care how hard it is or how challenging it is.

I want it to be hard because I know everybody else is not going to do it so I've just been able to take on the most challenging things that have come to my life and become masterful at them. and I'm still having fun doing that because every opportunity creates 10 other opportunities."

"I'm still having fun doing that because every opportunity creates 10 other opportunities."

DC GLENN

"I'M IN A PERPETUAL STATE OF PREPARATION RIGHT NOW"

And this lead us not directly to the commercial, but how that one small thing opened up other doors fo Dc.

" I did that during the Geico commercial because we were in a pandemic and I couldn't go do shows. So I was like well, try to find a publicist to do acting and you know get your acting going and all that. They didn't want to work with me because they didn't know how to do the commercial or they were just the covert thing. So I was like you know what, I'm gonna be my own publicist and I joined the organization called Public Relations Society of America (PRSA).So for two days i'm in a zoom chat with the ceo of this pr firm and I raised my hand and asked "Like is press release relevant?" They're like yeah. So I'm like, well I'm kind of featured in a Geico commercial called "Scoop! There it is!" and I'm looking at the chat it's like "Oh my god, what is he doing here that's not him." That just blew up the entire zoom call. The ceo comes back on and she's like of course that that press release is going to work. She gave me the breath of her experience in 10 minutes, and it changed my life forever. It's the reason that you and I are talking right now."

Seeing how people react, getting my story together ,breaking down analogies, making people understand where I come from. Making people see inspiring all these things. Even like it's therapy for me because I figure things out. I know where I want to be and where I want to go. What I want to do."

 Now before I let Dc go I had to ask one real entertainment question. So with your 10 things you have going on, what exactly are you working on that you can share?

"I think there's like three things I can't say anything about cause I'm under nda. But I'm an actor right and you know I have three tv shows co-starring. Three tv shows, one movie and I've got to audition constantly. So I'm a working actor here in Atlanta. I also do voiceover right. So I'm presenting at the voice-over awards and it's an honor that I just cherish. I'll be in New York at the Guggenheim. I'm gonna be with so many different people in the industry. I've worked hard for those things. I'm also into crypto.

But Dc didn't stop at just where he went to learn how to be his publicist, he added more value and depth. Going into how doing interviews has helped him.

"Like I said, I'm in a perpetual state of preparation right now. I do three or five of these a day because they serve so many different avenues for me. It kills 14 birds with one stone. I'm practicing articulation for voice-over. I'm practicing storytelling for acting. I'm practicing, you know, meeting new people, networking.

I'm putting out a lot of nfts, and got a metaverse play. That's what I'm working on. So you know I'm constantly doing things. Geico just gave us an ice cream that we're trying to launch in the spring. I'm doing nba halftime shows. I just finished two Thanksgiving Day Parades. Right like the sheer amount of things that I get to do, it's just astounding. But I set it up that way because I want to do a little bit of a bunch of things I like as opposed to one thing. And that's all I do. So that's how I fasten my life and that's how I love to learn and hustle and just create these opportunities for myself."

To connect with Dc Glenn he has made it simple to be found. As a master of SEO you can find him across all social media as **@DCGlenn** for Tag Team **@tagteamwhoop**
As it was an honor and privilege to speak to DC for this one of a kind interview . We at Trient Press want to thank him for his time and such a wonderful interview.

The Self-Publishing Guru Shares

BY: M.L.RUSCSAK

Book Interview

INSIGHTFUL MARKETING TIPS FOR NEW AUTHORS

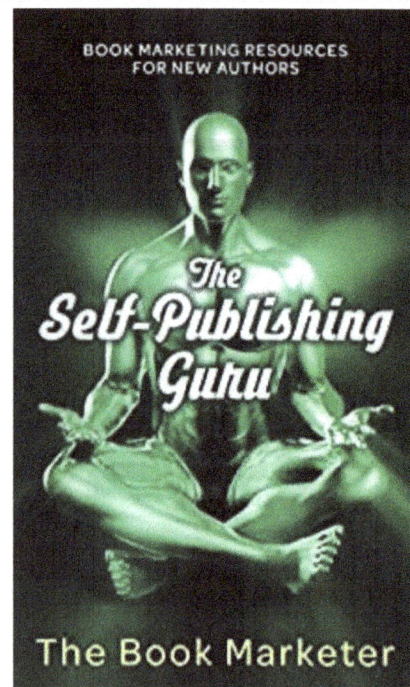

While having an agent can help some authors publish their books, it isn't necessary for all authors to find success in the publishing industry. New authors should consider taking advantage of the many marketing resources offered by self-publishing gurus who have been where they are and have learned what it takes to succeed in today's book market. An author's success doesn't just depend on the quality of their book, but also the steps they take after its publication to get the word out about their work.k.

IS BOOK MARKETING SOMETHING I NEED TO LEARN?

The truth is, if you want to be a successful author, then yes. If you want to sell more books, then yes. Book marketing is an essential part of being a self-published author and it's something that every author should know how to do well. Before we get into specific book marketing tips, it's helpful to understand just what book marketing entails. Book marketing isn't just a series of spammy tweets or newsletter blasts—it encompasses public relations (i.e., convincing people that your book is newsworthy), branding (for yourself and your books), content creation (writing and publishing articles about your book) and actually selling books directly through email outreach, social media groups and direct contact with bloggers and other authors in your genre.

" The best book marketers are people who love books "

Who is a good book marketer?

The best book marketers are people who love books and love to share them with other people. They become a successful book marketer because it's what they want to do, not because it's a business opportunity. You can't teach someone how to be enthusiastic about books; that enthusiasm is inherent in most good book marketers. A successful self-publisher does all of their marketing themselves rather than outsourcing, using any opportunity—the positive or negative—to generate interest in their book. Perhaps most importantly, a good self-publisher doesn't give up after one failed marketing attempt and continues to think outside of conventional methods of promotion while searching out new avenues that are likely to generate more success.

Which Book Marketing Tools Are Most

This is a great question, but there isn't one definitive answer. Each author will have their own book marketing strategy, their own strengths and weaknesses, and their own preferences when it comes to how they like to work. Tools should be chosen based on your strengths—the ones you feel most comfortable using—and on how you prefer to work. For example, maybe you're a social media guru or maybe you don't enjoy updating your Facebook page. There is no right or wrong way when it comes to book marketing tools, as long as you are doing what works best for you and your goals (which should include sales).

Such as, If you're writing crime thrillers and are hoping to be picked up by one of the big publishing houses, you need to research what publishers currently publish books like yours. Then it's down to creating a great book that will hopefully get them excited enough to buy it. At that point, most publishing houses have their own in-house marketing team who will work on promoting your book. But if you've self-published or if you're just starting out as an author looking for another avenue through which to sell your books—for example, if you want to create multiple streams of income from writing—you'll want additional tools at your disposal.

17
INSTAGRAM
Book Promotion
Ideas From Publishers

For more tips you'll have to pick up the book. Now available on Amazon
The Self-Publishing Guru: Book Marketing Resources for New Authors

Discover.Live

BY: M.L.RUSCSAK

Travel with Trient Press

Virtual Travel connecting friends and families since 2018

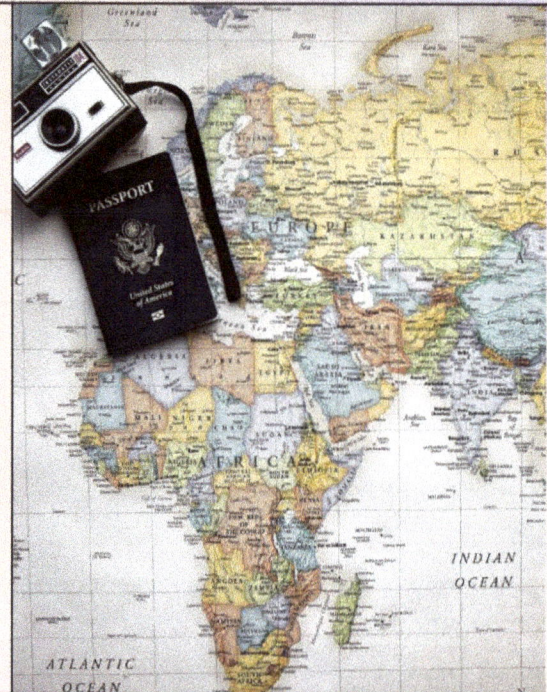

Unique Experiences with custom itineraries are their specialty. Joinn in frm up to 3 location for each tour

Ask about tours for homeschooling or groups

Book today
https://www.discover.live

Discover.Live Virtual Travel, Unique Travel Experiences

What if you could visit the pyramids of Egypt and walk the streets of Paris without leaving your living room? You can with Discover Live Virtual Travel, which offers virtual travel experiences that are as authentic as they are diverse, as memorable as they are affordable. They take you around the world with our most popular destinations, or you can customize your own itinerary. They offer the ability to see landmarks from unique perspectives and experience the cultures of these destinations as if you were there in person.Visit them today to learn more about our exciting vacation packages.

Personalized Tours

Plan a trip that's uniquely yours. We call it Discover Live virtual travel and it makes planning vacations easy. Once you tell us where you want to go and we take care of everything else. With personalized tours from your itinerary all done at an exceptional value —They make every moment on your virtual vacation count. From culture and cuisine to art and architecture Discover Live is changing how people explore live their passions by discovering new places in real time with virtual travel experiences to destinations around the world.

Local Experts

Get a Personalized Tour Experience of Your Choice: Discover Live is an innovative new platform that offers its members exclusive access to world-class travel experiences. There are plenty of ways for travelers to enjoy exploring different cities and countries around the world; however, you can't always depend on what others have done in order to get a truly one-of-a-kind experience. This is where Discover Live steps in. The platform works with local experts in various locations throughout Europe and Austrialia to provide guests with authentic cultural exchange and personal experiences that you won't find anywhere else. You can even choose which city your expert guides you through based on their expertise rather than trying to decide from countless options online.

Having experienced one of their many tours as seen in this excessive video it is well worth the time and money. Bringing us all together from across the globe and experiencing all that the would has to offer.

Book today https://www.discover.live/

For the full story visit www.Trientpressmagazine.com

with a special video tour.

MI Ruscsak

The Power of SEO and why it's Important to Your Business

Before we understand the how and the why of SEO, we first needs to know what it is. In the simplest of terms search engine optimization (SEO) marketing is just like its name implies – it's about increasing the visibility of your site in search engines such as Google and Bing when people look for information related to your business. It's also called search engine marketing, but since that term refers to the broader concept of promoting your website on search engines and includes paid advertising, we'll use SEO marketing in this article to describe strategies that are free or low-cost.

I have carefully broken down SEO into four key areas to better help you and your business succeed.

Why Search Engine Optimization is so important?

With millions of websites competing for visibility in search engines, you need to market your business effectively if you want to get noticed. Unfortunately, there's no one size fits all solution here — every business is different and has its own set of goals. But one thing's for sure: ignoring search engine optimization will make it almost impossible to grow your business fast. Today, people are more likely to do research on a product before making a purchase decision. In fact, more than 80% of consumers use search engines when looking for information about a product or service they're considering buying.

This is why search engine optimization (SEO) has become increasingly important in today's business world. So... What is SEO? In simple terms, it means improving your site to increase its visibility when people search for your product or service on a search engine such as Google. For example, if you sell blue widgets, you want to make sure that when people search for blue widgets your site appears at or near the top of their list. You can improve your ranking by working with an SEO expert to ensure that your site is optimized with key words related to what you do and how you do it. There are many free tips available online, but it pays in both time and money to hire a professional.

What We Can Do To Achieve Better Visibility?

In many business schools, students spend years building tools and understanding how to create a user experience that attracts people looking for a search engine marketing solution. In essence, they're helping people like you find your next customer.First by creating an effective website and telling your story in a compelling way, you increase your chances of getting new customers or clients. It doesn't matter what industry you're in -- virtually everyone needs more clients or customers (the fact that you're reading this post means you do). There are many companies out there that can help with search engine optimization (SEO) to improve your visibility on search engines like Google and Bing. but before you dive into just any SEO mastering company, you first need to understand what you need as a business and what your clients needs from you. Please do your research before making any commitment with any company.

SEO Marketing is a must!

Sample strategy for achieving better visibility

Use keyword-rich, accurate titles, headers and image descriptions. Keep your text scannable (by using subheads and bullet points). Use social media to build an audience for your site or content. Get backlinks from relevant sites to increase visibility on search engines. We'll go over some strategies for doing all of these things in a minute. But first let's ask why you'd want any of that in the first place? Your product is great! Why aren't people buying it? The most likely answer is that they don't know about it. And even if they do know about it, chances are they don't know how great it is because you haven't told them yet.

Optimize your site for keywords related to your business. If you sell custom-made bags, include words like handbags and satchels in product descriptions, even if those words aren't already relevant to your business. Ensure that every page on your site has a unique title tag, description, and image (use Google search to make sure you don't repeat yourself). You can go even further by making small changes or updates to content that already exists on your site—this is an easy way to boost your content quality score on sites like Alexa and Google Search Console. By tracking keyword positions using a service like Ahrefs, you can easily see which pages of your site need work.

Also if you use site builders such as Wix, Godaddy or wordpress they have built in analytics so you can see where your traffic comes from and which post or pages are getting the most traffic. After all higher traffic means higher conversion rates.

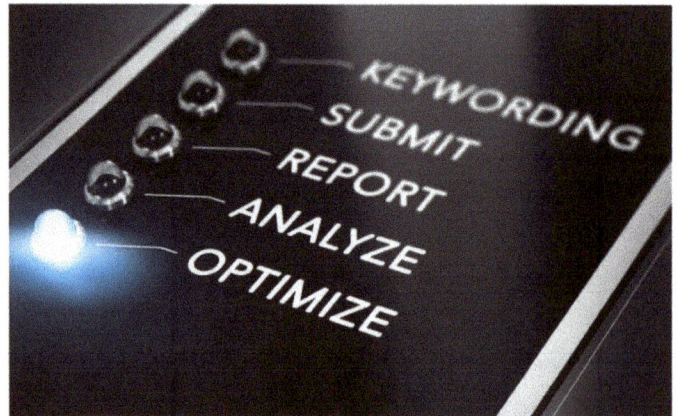

Advantages of an optimized website

Optimizing your website for search engines does have some distinct advantages. By increasing your site's visibility, you'll boost traffic, and that can translate into more interest in your products or services, which can lead to increased sales. It's a process known as traffic generation; you start by targeting those people most likely to purchase from you and then entice them to do so.

People will be able to find your business on search engines, helping you get more leads. The higher ranking on search engine results pages (SFRPs) leads to increased traffic and sales. For example, a study by WordStream found that people using organic listings had a 55% higher chance of converting than people using paid ads. And according to Moz's State of Inbound report , 69% of respondents who used organic search in their buying process said they converted in 2015.

Final Thoughts

Even if you're a small business that operates in just one area, SEO marketing is still important. It provides your business with an increased online presence and can lead to new clients from other areas. If you don't have any customers yet, it can help attract them to your business. Even if you have a brick-and-mortar shop and no plans to move into e-commerce anytime soon, a little bit of effort into SEO marketing can go a long way toward increasing your visibility. You never know what opportunities might come along as a result!

It goes without saying that I think every entrepreneur should put in the hard work to learn how to do his or her own marketing. It's one of those things you'll probably never get 100% right, but if you want a serious leg up, it's one area where putting in your own effort can really pay off. There are few tools more powerful than search engine optimization, and it will be very difficult for any future competitors to beat you in that space. Your online presence is key for your business and having a major advantage there will pay dividends for years to come. Stay tuned for my next post on getting people from your site into your sales funnel!

Attract your market

Just a few websites to help with your SEO

- https://marketerhire.com/
- JoshFechter.com
- https://www.seo.com/
- https://www.socialseo.com/
- https://www.smartsites.com/
- https://ignitevisibility.com/
- https://victoriousseo.com/
- https://disruptiveadvertising.com/
- https://www.digitalsilk.com/

For M.L.Ruscsak, the world is her playground. Always seeing things with her own vision and never looking back on yesterday. Bringing it all into her fantasy world one page at a time.

Victorious PR

🌐 **https://victoriouspr.com/**

✉️ **support@victoriouspr.com**

📞 **(702) 718- 5821**

Don't take our word for it

"Literal GOLD! If your clients don't know you, they aren't going to trust you and Victoria has helped me overcome that and so much more. She got me on Yahoo Finance and it absolutely blew my mind! I've been over the moon with the quality of work."

Bao Le | CEO of Bao Digital

Real Estate:
Praise from the
Real Estate Industry

Victoria did amazing things. Uncovered things that I never even thought of, like going to different publications and getting us sent to those publications with stories and was able to get us sent to the RJ and which is a huge local newspaper. And I got a lot of personal private messages. She uncovered a lot of ways to get our brand and my face out in front of people that I would have never imagined I could have been in front of.

Coltyn Simmons Founder of Custom Fit Real Estate

Praise from the
Entrepreneur Industry

"You've done a great job, Victoria. Thank you so much. All these articles were wonderful and I love having the logos behind my name now it just gives us more credibility."

Krista Mashore Coach, Best Selling Author

FEATURED IN:

inman Forbes Entrepreneur yahoo! finance

abc TODAY GSD mode FOX NEWS

📷 thevictoriakennedy 📘 @thevictoriuspr 🐦 @GoVictorias 💼 victoriajkennedy

VICTORIOUS PR

What We Do

We create Industry Leaders
We help businesses be seen as the #1 Authority in their niche.

Your next giant leap leans on more than metrics, channels, and platforms alone. It requires a pitch-perfect mix of strategic precision, deeply human thinking, creative prowess, and some love.

Victorious PR is a global agency working across fields to build brands that attract, brands that offer a unique position, and brands that effect real change in the world.

REAL ESTATE

Although the real estate mantra is "location,location, location," we're all about "public relations, publick relations, pulic relations." What good is a great loaction's availablity, if no one knows about it?

ENTREPRENEURS

No matter what stage of business you're in, know that your story matters. We put you in the forefront to get the right notoeriety you deserve.

AND SO MUCH MORE...

One Of Our Success Stories

While most people can't handle one job, Farrah Ali has three. During the day she is a fulltime insurance professional, at night she is a full time investor and she is the author of Diaries of a Female Real Estate Investor. To top it all off, the most important job for her is being a single mother to her two kids.

Farrah has been a crucial piece to the growth of Chicago REIA since the beginning. Her journey with investing started in June of 2014, now just four short years later she is at twenty-five rental properties, one flip, and eight wholesale deals.

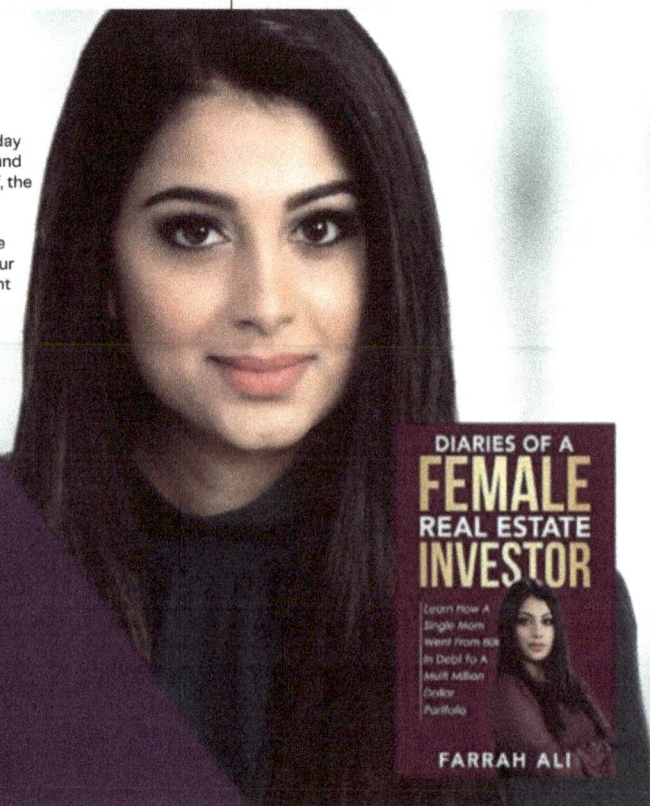

FARRAH ALI

Real Estate Investor, Entrepreneur & Author
www.farrahali.org

THE ALL-IMPORTANT HOOK

BY SHERI CHAPMAN

How do you create the hook?

Market your book

Although all elements of story writing are important, the hook is one of the most important aspects. Without it, your book will not sell.

If you're new to writing, you may find yourself wanting to explain the beginning so you can get to "the good stuff" where you'll hook your readers. This is a good process... in your rough draft. In your final copy, get rid of it. Begin with "the good stuff". You can always create flashbacks to explain processes or backstories later. You must get the interest up in the reader or they simply will not read your book.

So, how do you create the hook? Your beginning must be interesting and original. Start with an exciting moment. A great place to begin is in the middle of action. Paint a picture to lure your readers with: a scene of conflict, a monumental moment, an unusual or intriguing situation, compelling narration, a character is feeling great emotion, surprise about something, or an ironic or dreaded situation. I'm sure there are more, but these are safe bets to use for a hook.

Remember, let your readers figure out things in your story. You want to make them wonder, so don't explain everything. You also need to keep the level of interest up throughout your plot. Your story is not about one fantastic moment, it's about building a relationship between your story and the readers to keep them hooked throughout your entire plot.

Examples of hooks:

Action

I darted down a narrow alley and squatted behind the barrel. Did he see me? Did he know where I was? My breath hissed rhythmically although I quietly tried to control it. I squinted from behind my hiding spot. There. He was standing with his back to the alleyway. His muscular profile was silhouetted in the deepening light. Slowly, he turned. I held my breath and screwed my eyes closed as the crunch of gravel grew closer.

Build the Emotion and Set the Scene

BUILD THE EMOTION

UNUSUAL/INTRIGUING SITUATION

There it was again. A brilliant flash of scarlet and gold erupted within the dancing flames. It was like an artist added a subtle twist of color that most wouldn't notice. I leaned in closer and stared into the pit. A bright spark began to outline a crimson egg that was so hot it glowed like a burning coal. I jumped when it rolled towards me.

Compelling Narration

Kaitlin knew they shouldn't cross the river. Not today. The river was up, and there was too much weight in the wagon. In addition, the oxen were lathered and their heads drooped. She stared with wide eyes at the angry waves. Unfortunately, the decision when to cross wasn't hers to make, and her father always pushed limits.

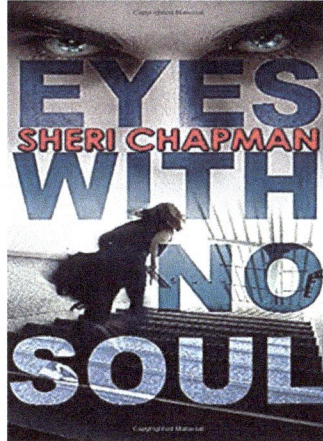

SHERI CHAPMAN — EYES WITH NO SOUL

EX. 1

"I told you to not bring home another dog. This is it. I've had enough!"

Stan Oolong looked down at his wife of fifteen months. His arms were crossed and his chest was inflated. His mouth was turned down and his brows rumpled over his clear blue eyes.

"Stan, I need a new male," Livi said. She flipped her dark hair over her shoulder. "I breed dogs for a living. It's not like I'm taking charity cases."

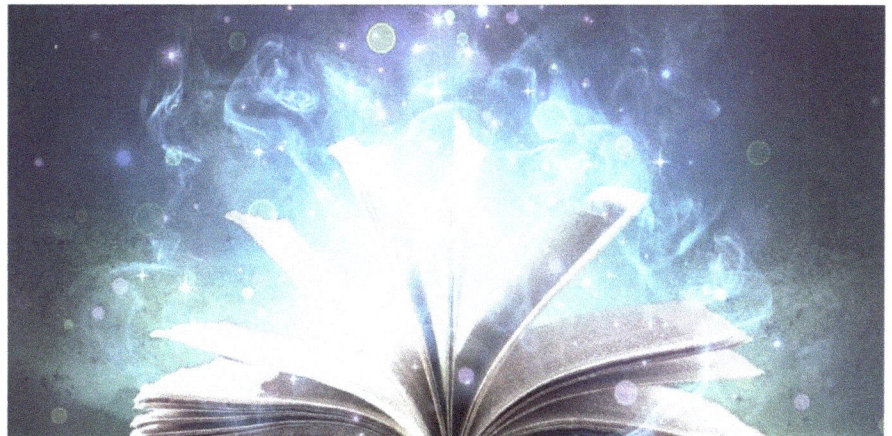

EX.2

Rubin's hand was suspended in the air over his gun. His legs trembled and a chill ran up his spine despite the hot sun.

"I ain't putin' up with no cheaters," the big man said, "but I'll let ya walk away."

Rubin swallowed. "I wasn't cheatin' and I ain't leaving my winnings."

"Ya sure?" the slinger growled. His grizzled hair stuck to his skin and his eyes tracked Rubin's movements with the awareness of a tiger.

A Monumental Moment

The shark swam closer. I could see the rows of deadly sharp teeth. Normally in the presence of a dangerous animal, I would have frozen, but it was nearly impossible to do forty feet down with an air tank on my back and respirator blowing bubbles at regular intervals. Not to mention buoyancy control with my increased heart rate. Still, I was excited. This is what I've waited my whole life to do.

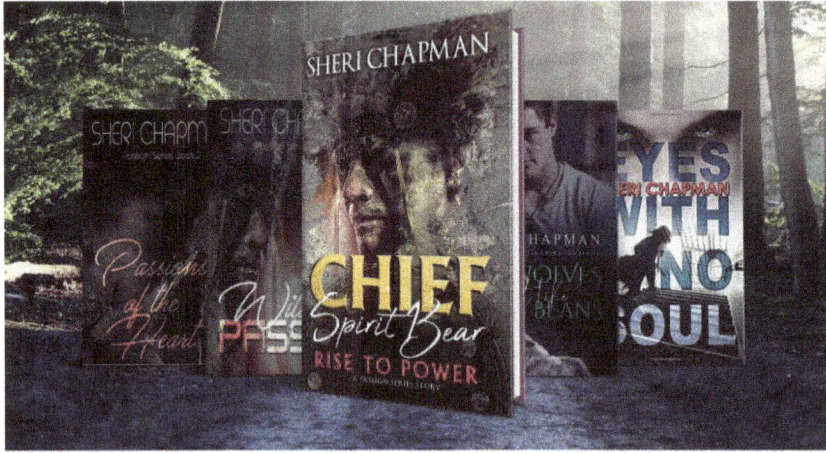

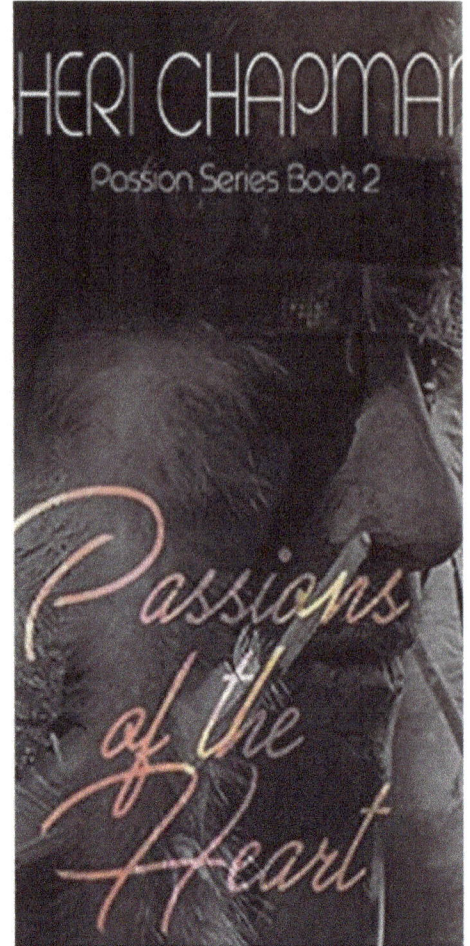

Great Emotion

Ann looked around the room. Her heart pounded in her chest, and she couldn't catch her breath, even with the help of the machine. Alone. She was all alone. No one would be coming to help. The risk was too great.

A nurse entered with a syringe full of a clear liquid. Ann reached out a hand, gasping for breath.

"It's okay, hun," the nurse said with a kind smile and sad eyes. "We're going to sedate you. You're just having a little panic attack. You'll be okay."

Surprise

Danny shuffled to the door. A tall blond kid was standing outside with a strangely wrapped box.

"Billy?"

"I brought you a present for your birthday," Billy said. "Dad said it's gonna be a blast."

"Thanks, Billy. To tell you the truth, I didn't think you'd come. Honestly, I didn't think you liked me."

Billy shuffled his feet but didn't say anything as he stood in front of him.

"It's a shame you couldn't make it to my party," Danny continued.

"Oh, it's okay. I wanted to give you this in private. Tell me what you think it is." The tall boy handed Danny the box.

"Um..." Danny held the gift to his ear. "Something mechanical? It's making a slight noise. Is it... ticking?"

"Kind of, yes," Billy said, grinning.

"Well, I've got to go. Have fun."

"Don't you want to see me open up the gift you brought?"

"Not really."

Ironic/Dreaded Situation

"What in the hell is this?" the inmate yelled.

"It's your last meal, man," the guard said with a smirk and a wink.

"I didn't order this. Who would order bread and water for their last meal?" The man behind the bars looked up at the patrolman.

"You better eat up if you don't want to be hungry." The officer's grin was wider now.

"You've got to be kidding me!" The inmate flipped his tray.

"Do you think I care if you get a meal to enjoy after what you've done?" The guard laughed. "I have to admit, though. That steak you ordered was cooked perfectly. Just like I like."

Sheri Chapman loves life and laughing, but you couldn't tell it by her work - from historical romances, suspense, dark fiction, or horror stories. A former teacher of thirty years and mother to four grown daughters, you can follow her on Facebook, Instagram and Twitter to find links to her books.

CALLSIGN, GHOST
The Haunting Shot

Together, can they find the killer?

R.B.
carr

TRIENT PRESS

Trient Press

R.B.
CARR

Trient Press

THE CRITICAL FIRST DAY

How many times have you witnessed the Non-Welcome Wagon on someone's first day at your company, or during your own corporate transitions?

This critical first day is handled so poorly at a majority of companies, that often the new employee's opinion of the organization can never be fully repaired. Today, write on the cover of your Personnel Manual, "Make First Days Great!" If the new teammate's first day in your company, charity or civic group is not carefully scripted to be exemplary, the remainder of the relationship will be weaker for it (remember the rules on first impressions).

Yet, how is this most-critical task handled at most companies today? First, they get a lucky break. The all-star performer, Joe, whom they've been recruiting for two years goes through a difficult corporate merger, feels unloved, and now takes them up on their offer to join the company. They finalize all the details and schedule Joe's first day two weeks down the road. Then, they go back to managing the sales problems in the Cleveland office.

That fateful first day, Joe is up early and nervous. His wife, Susan, selects him the perfect tie, and he promises to tell her all about his amazing day over a celebration dinner tonight. Joe says one last time, "I hope I made the right decision." Susan smooches him on the cheek and tells him, "I'm so proud of you."

Joe arrives at the office. The busy receptionist lets him know that his boss is in Cleveland and directs him to take a seat. After forty-five minutes, the HR assistant greets him and leads him to an empty cubicle. His office is not ready, and she's not sure which one is his, anyways. She tells him, "Everyone's in meetings today, so please read the Personnel Handbook. Sorry it's 300 pages, but we have a lot of rules." Il talk.

Joe makes sure not to bother anyone. He skips lunch because he's not sure of the office protocol. But he does consider sneaking out to the corner tavern for a few drinks while he contemplates what he has just done to his promising career. At 5:05 he slides out the back. Susan rushes to the door to greet him and find out every detail of his amazing day. Joe sulks into the house and says, "It was fine, but I sure hope it gets better tomorrow." The two sit quietly over dinner wondering what the future holds.

Or instead, if Joe was joining our team of A-Players at one of our organizations, here is how we've always attempted to flip this script. First, I send out an internal email the morning before Joe's first day explaining the new position and providing a little information about our new teammate, so everyone was in the loop and prepared to give a warm welcome.

Joe walks into the office wearing that perfect tie, the receptionist jumps up, introduces themselves, and gets Joe a coffee and a danish to welcome him to the office. Our best receptionist ever was Justin, a 24-year-old good-looking guy who talked his parents into helping him buy some new business suits. He would leap to his feet, smile, shake hands, and treat all visitors like Kings and Queens. I can't count how many compliments we received about Justin.

Back to Joe. His new assistant, Robert, hurries out to greet him and lead him to his new office. Along the walk, Robert stops at each desk and introduces Joe to the Team. Each associate puts their call on hold for the greeting and mentions one familiarity, "I see our kids are in the same soccer league!" and "Oh no! Not another Georgetown grad in the firm!"
an employer?"

Over Joe's new office hangs a welcome banner, balloons float inside, and on the table is a gift basket with New Zealand sauvignon blanc (How did they know?). Two goody bags for the kids hold company t-shirts, hats, and treats. Lunch is scheduled with three members of his department. At two o'clock Joe meets with his new boss and receives three projects in desperate need of his brilliance. Suddenly, it's six PM, and Joe remembers that he promised a special dinner with the family.

At the door, he's greeted by an excited Susan. Joe says, "Let me tell you about this amazing firm!" Susan interrupts, "Wait until you first hear about my day! Two nice women from your company surprised me at my office with a welcome basket of goodies, balloons, and my favorite cabernet! You must have told them! I was the hit of the office. Everyone spent the day asking me about your new company!"

Joe, Susan and the kids have a special dinner and have that feeling inside they can't quite describe, except that everything just feels right.

Just how many people do you think Joe and Susan told about their amazing first day and this wonderful company? Just about everyone who would listen, twice! Always remember that everyone just wants to be inspired. Everyone craves to be part of something special, and the critical first day sets the tone for the entire mission. The First Day Strategy is so easy, costs almost nothing, and provides a priceless reward.

"He who has a why to live for, can bear with almost any how." - Nietzsche

For more bussiness blogs and advice visit : https://www.jamviewsblog.com/
Article by : Jeff Martinovich

Enjoy a international delight !

POTICA
by Chef Dennis Littley

PREP TIME
1 HR 20 MINS
COOK TIME
40 MINS
TOTAL TIME
2 HRS

Bring ataste of Eastern European Cuisine to your own home.

INGREDIENTS (4 SERVINGS):

INGREDIENTS:

BREAD
½ CUP GRANULATED SUGAR
1 TEASPOON SALT
¼ CUP BUTTER
1 CUP HOT MILK
2 PACKAGES ACTIVE DRY YEAST
¼ CUP WARM WATER (105-115F)
2 EGGS
4.5 CUPS UNSIFTED ALL-PURPOSE FLOUR
FILLING
3 EGGS
4 CUPS (1LB) WALNUTS, FINELY CHOPPED
1 CUP LIGHT BROWN SUGAR , PACKED
⅓ CUP BUTTER , MELTED
1 ½ TEASPOONS CINNAMON (I OMIT DUE TO ALLERGIES)
1 TEASPOON VANILLA BEAN PASTE OR EXTRACT

Enjoy!

INSTRUCTIONS:

STIR SUGAR, SALT AND ¼ CUP BUTTER INTO HOT MILK. COOL TO LUKEWARM. (A DROP ON YOUR WRIST WON'T FEEL HOT)

SPRINKLE YEAST OVER WARM WATER IN A LARGE BOWL. STIR TO DISSOLVE. STIR IN LUKEWARM MILK MIXTURE.

ADD 2 EGGS AND 2.5 CUPS FLOUR. BEAT WITH A WOODEN SPOON UNTIL SMOOTH.

GRADUALLY BEAT IN REMAINING 2 CUPS FLOUR; KNEAD WITH HAND UNTIL THE DOUGH IS STIFF ENOUGH TO LEAVE SIDE OF BOWL.

PLACE DOUGH IN A LIGHTLY GREASED LARGE BOWL. TURN DOUGH OVER – GREASED SIDE UP – AND COVER WITH A TOWEL.

LET RISE IN WARM PLACE (85F) FREE FROM DRAFTS, UNTIL DOUBLED IN SIZE – ABOUT AN HOUR.

MAKE FILLING – IN A MEDIUM BOWL BEAT EGGS SLIGHTLY, ADD NUTS, BROWN SUGAR, ⅓ CUP MELTED BUTTER, CINNAMON AND VANILLA. STIR AND SET ASIDE.

WHEN DOUGH HAS RISEN, PUNCH DOWN. ON A LIGHTLY FLOURED SURFACE, TURN DOUGH OUT, COVER WITH BOWL AND LET REST FOR 10 MINUTES.

ROLL THE DOUGH OUT TO A 30X20" RECTANGLE.
SPREAD WITH FILLING, TO 1 INCH FROM EDGE.

STARTING FROM WIDE SIDE – ROLL UP TIGHTLY – JELLYROLL STYLE. SEAL BY PINCHING EDGES OF DOUGH WITH FINGERS.

ON A LARGE GREASED COOKIE SHEET OR SEASONED BAKING STONE, FORM ROLL INTO A LARGE COIL.

LET RISE IN A WARM PLACE (85F), COVER WITH TOWEL, FOR ONE HOUR. PREHEAT OVEN TO 350F. BRUSH WITH 2 TABLESPOONS MELTED BUTTER.

BAKE 35-40 MINUTES UNTIL GOLDEN.

COOL ON WIRE RACK. MAKES A WHOPPING 4-POUND LOAF!

The Perfect Holiday Cookie!

These easy kolachy cookies are a staple in many Eastern European countries

MY FAMILY REIPIE

CREAM CHEESE KOLACKY

6 OUNCES CREAM CHEESE

1 CUP BUTTER, SOFTENED

1 1/4 CUP CAKE FLOUR

1/2 CUP ANY FLAVOR FRUIT JAM

1/3 CUP CONFECTIONERS' SUGAR FOR DECORATION

MIX CREAM CHEESE AND BUTTER UNTIL SMOOTH. SHIFT FLOWER BEFOR ADDING FLOUR SLOWLY UNTIL WELL BLENDED. SHAPE INTO A BALL AND CHILL OVERNIGHT OR FOR SEVERAL HOURS.

PREHEAT OVEN TO 350 DEGREES F (180 DEGREES C). ROLL DOUGH OUT 1/8 INCH THICK ON A FLOURED PASTRY BOARD. CUT INTO 2 1/2 INCH SQUARES AND PLACE 1/2 TSP (APPROX) OF JAM OR PRESERVES. OVERLAP OPPOSITE CORNERS AND PINCH TOGETHER. PLACE ON UNGREASED COOKIE SHEETS.

BAKE FOR 10 TO 12 MINUTES IN THE PREHEATED OVEN. COOL. SPRINKLE LIGHTLY WITH CONFECTIONER'S SUGAR.

MY FAMILY REIPIE

CHRISTMAS PINWHEEL COOKIES

4 CUPS ALL-PURPOSE FLOUR
1 TEASPOON BAKING POWDER
1/4 TEASPOON BAKING SODA
1 TEASPOON SALT
1 1/3 CUPS BUTTER
1 CUP PACKED BROWN SUGAR
2/3 CUP WHITE SUGAR
2 EGGS, BEATEN
1 1/2 TEASPOONS VANILLA EXTRACT
1 DROP RED FOOD COLORING, OR AS NEEDED
1 DROP GREEN FOOD COLORING, OR AS NEEDED

SIFT THE FLOUR, BAKING POWDER, BAKING SODA, AND SALT TOGETHER INTO A BOWL. RESIFT AGAIN INTO ANOTHER BOWL.
BEAT THE BUTTER WITH THE BROWN AND WHITE SUGARS IN A MIXING BOWL UNTIL LIGHT AND FLUFFY. BEAT IN THE EGGS AND VANILLA UNTIL SMOOTH. GRADUALLY STIR IN THE FLOUR MIXTURE UNTIL EVENLY BLENDED. GATHER THE DOUGH INTO A BALL, AND DIVIDE INTO TWO EQUAL PARTS. PLACE ONE HALF IN A SECOND BOWL.
ADD RED FOOD COLORING TO THE DOUGH IN ONE BOWL, AND GREEN FOOD COLORING TO THE DOUGH IN THE OTHER BOWL. USE A FORK OR WOODEN SPOON TO BLEND THE FOOD COLORING INTO THE DOUGH UNTIL EVENLY BLENDED. ADD ADDITIONAL DROPS OF FOOD COLORING TO MAKE THE DESIRED SHADE.
ROLL OUT THE RED DOUGH TO 1/4 INCH (5MM) THICKNESS. ROLL OUT THE GREEN DOUGH TO 1/4 INCH (5MM) THICKNESS, AND PLACE ON TOP OF THE RED DOUGH. BEGINNING ON ONE EDGE, ROLL THE DOUGHS TO MAKE A LOG SO THE TWO COLORS SPIRAL INSIDE EACH OTHER. WRAP THE LOG IN WAXED PAPER, THEN IN A COTTON TOWEL, AND REFRIGERATE AT LEAST 8 HOURS.
PREHEAT OVEN TO 400 DEGREES F (200 DEGREES C). LIGHTLY GREASE 2 BAKING SHEETS.
UNWRAP THE DOUGH LOG, AND PLACE ON A CLEAN, LIGHTLY FLOURED SURFACE. SLICE THE LOG INTO ROUNDS 1/8 INCH (3 MM) THICK, AND PLACE ON PREPARED BAKING SHEETS.
BAKE IN PREHEATED OVEN UNTIL SET, 5 TO 6 MINUTES. WATCH CAREFULLY TO PREVENT EDGES FROM BROWNING. REMOVE FROM OVEN, AND COOL ON RACKS.

MY FAMILY REIPIE

CREAM CHEESE FILLING.
BOTH RECIPES TRADIONALLY HAVE THE CREAM CHEESE FILLING

NGREDIENTSINGREDIENT CHECKLIST

8 OUNCES CREAM CHEESE (SOFTENED)

¼ CUP GRANULATED SUGAR

1 EGG YOLK

½ TEASPOON PURE VANILLA EXTRACT

¼ TEASPOON GROUND CARDAMOM

⅛ TEASPOON GROUND NUTMEG

A PINCH OF SALT

IN A MEDIUM BOWL MIX THE EGG YOLK, SUGAR AND VANILLA. SLOWLY ADD CREAM CHEESE UNTIL FULLY INCOPERATED THEN ANDD DRY INGREDANTS. MIX TILL SMOOTH.

PLEASE NOTE YOU MAY HAVE TO PLAY AROUND WITH THE MIXTURE TILL YOU HAVE THE SMOOTHNESS AND SWEETNESS THAT YOU DESIRE.

FUNDING RESOURCES FOR ENTREPRENEURS

1. Angel Investors

If your business is a start-up, you may have access to a few different funding options. The first is an angel investor, who is a person interested in investing in a company as an entrepreneur. Angel investors can provide a one-time investment to help get the business off the ground or offer continuous support as the needs of the business grow and change. The difference between an angel investor and another type of investor is the focus on the success of the business, rather than reaping a big profit.

If you're interested in this option, try using online resources like AngelList or Gust to find potential investors. These websites focus on connecting small business owners with angel investors. Gust functions like a social network, allowing you to build relationships and interact with investors. AngelList is more complicated, but you can set up a profile with an activity feed, which investors can view. All start-ups and potential investors registered on these sites have gone through a vetting process to make sure they're legitimate.

Angel.co

gust.com

angelinvestmentnetwork.co.uk

angelcapitalassociation.org

Funded.com

angelforum.org

Envestors.co.uk

goldenseeds.com (for women only)

FUNDING RESOURCES FOR ENTREPRENEURS

Venture capital
The most common investment option for small businesses is venture capital. Venture capitalists will typically invest in companies with the potential for long-term growth. On the investor's side, the risk is high, because the growth is generally based on perception and projections. Investors continue to offer venture capital because of the potential for higher-than-average returns. For start-up companies with limited history, obtaining traditional funding is more challenging, so venture capital is a funding option that is within easier reach.

Alta Partners

Sequoia Capital

Founder's Fund

Lightspeed Venture Partners

Susa Ventures

Atomico

Emergence Capital

First Round

FactoryMade

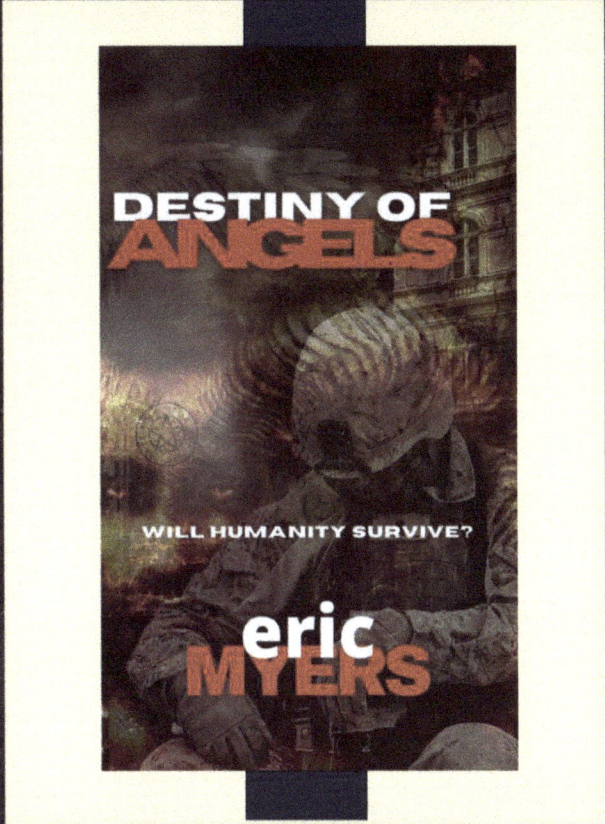

DESTINY OF
ANGELS

WILL HUMANITY SURVIVE?

eric
MYERS

Eric Myers

Trient Press

www.ingramcontent.com/pod-product-compliance
Lightning Source LLC
Chambersburg PA
CBHW041911220326
R18017300001B/R180173PG41597CBX00003B/1